HAUNTED PLACES
HAUNTED TOWNS

KENNY ABDO

Fly!
An Imprint of Abdo Zoom
abdobooks.com

abdobooks.com

Published by Abdo Zoom, a division of ABDO, P.O. Box 398166, Minneapolis, Minnesota 55439. Copyright © 2021 by Abdo Consulting Group, Inc. International copyrights reserved in all countries. No part of this book may be reproduced in any form without written permission from the publisher. Fly!™ is a trademark and logo of Abdo Zoom.

Printed in the United States of America, North Mankato, Minnesota.
052020
092020

Photo Credits: AP Images, Granger Collection, iStock, newscom, Shutterstock, ©Michael Gimenez p16 / CC BY-SA 3.0, ©Bex Walton p18 / CC BY 2.0
Production Contributors: Kenny Abdo, Jennie Forsberg, Grace Hansen
Design Contributors: Dorothy Toth, Neil Klinepier

Library of Congress Control Number: 2019956160

Publisher's Cataloging-in-Publication Data

Names: Abdo, Kenny, author.
Title: Haunted towns / by Kenny Abdo
Description: Minneapolis, Minnesota : Abdo Zoom, 2021 | Series: Haunted places | Includes online resources and index.
Identifiers: ISBN 9781098221348 (lib. bdg.) | ISBN 9781644944158 (pbk.) | ISBN 9781098222321 (ebook) | ISBN 9781098222819 (Read-to-Me ebook)
Subjects: LCSH: Haunted places--Juvenile literature. | Ghost towns--Juvenile literature. | Ghosts--Juvenile literature.
Classification: DDC 133.122--dc23

TABLE OF CONTENTS

Towns 4

The History 8

The Haunted 12

The Media 20

Glossary 22

Online Resources 23

Index 24

TOWNS

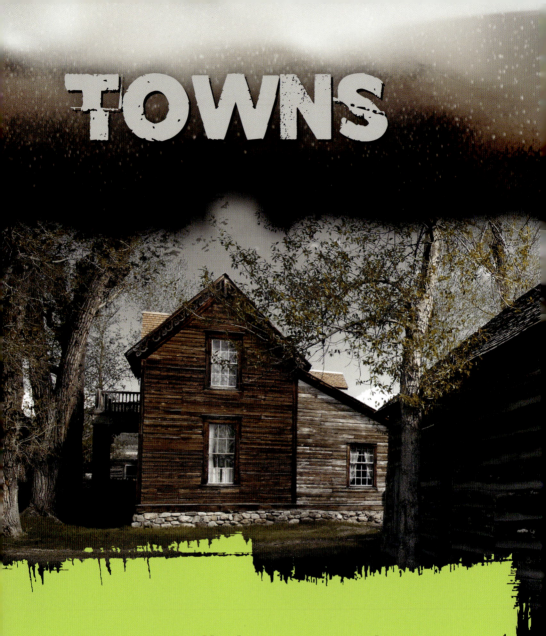

Towns usually have quaint houses, picket fences, and lemonade stands. For those haunted by their past residents, you will find a dark story at every **intersection**.

What was once lively and warm, towns filled with **paranormal** activity are places where **spirits** have hunkered down.

THE HISTORY

The word "town" comes from a few different places. The origin is shared with the Dutch word *tuin* and German word *zaun*. Both mean "enclosure."

Towns are communities where people have settled. Many haunted communities throughout the United States once began as small **settlements**.

Haunted towns have storied and creepy pasts, which is what make them the **eerie** places they are today.

THE HAUNTED

Shepherdstown has lots of **paranormal** activity. Ghost sightings have been reported in the West Virginia town, mainly at the Entler Hotel. Guests have heard the cries of a man killed there many years ago as their wakeup call.

Salem, Massachusetts, is most famous for the gruesome witch trials it held in the late 1600s. Today, many places in Salem are reportedly haunted. From certain homes, to movie theaters, and stores, the witches have more chaos to reign over the town.

A hurricane tore through Galveston, Texas in 1900, leaving more than 8,000 deceased residents. Today, homes and hotels are said to be haunted by **spirits** still looking for **refuge** from the hurricane.

Savannah, Georgia is a hot tourist draw of the south. Not just for its culture and beautiful architecture, but for its intense **supernatural** energy. Known for being "built on its dead," Savannah embraces its **spectral** residents with many ghost tours and public cemeteries.

Helltown in the Cuyahoga Valley in Ohio got its name for a devilish reason. Some say the town was overrun by **Satanists**, driving out the rest of the town's residents. Today, Helltown is empty, except for the ghosts of the past.

It can even get creepy beneath a town. The Shanghai Tunnels below Portland, Oregon are haunted by thousands of young men of the 19th century. They were drugged, carried through the tunnels, and sold to ship captains as slave labor.

THE MEDIA

From *Ghost Adventures* to *Destination Truth*, haunted towns have been investigated thoroughly for entertainment. There are several Facebook groups dedicated to studying ghostly towns as well.

You better hope your car never breaks down near a haunted town. The local ghosts do not take kindly to outsiders.

GLOSSARY

eerie – mysterious and frightening.

intersection – the point in which two roads meet.

paranormal – an occurrence beyond the scope of scientific understanding.

refuge – a place that provides shelter from harm.

Satanist – a member of a group who practices Satanism. They believe in the ideas and values of Satan.

settlement – a place where people have recently settled.

spectral – ghostly or unearthly.

spirit – a being that is not of this world, such as a ghost.

supernatural – a force beyond scientific logic and the laws of nature.

ONLINE RESOURCES

To learn more about haunted towns, please visit **abdobooklinks.com** or scan this QR code. These links are routinely monitored and updated to provide the most current information available.

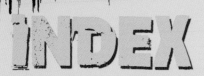

Destination Truth (TV show) 20

Georgia 16

Ghost Adventures (TV show) 20

Massachusetts 14

Ohio 17

Oregon 19

Satanism 17

Texas 15

United States 10, 13, 14, 15, 16, 17, 19

West Virginia 13

witches 14